Whose Birthday Is It?

Written and Created by:

Monica Fortune

Whose Birthday Is It?
Copyright © 2015 Monica Fortune

All rights reserved. No portion of this book may be reproduced, stored in a retrieval system, or transmitted in any form or by any means – electronic, mechanical, photocopy, recording, or any other – except for brief quotations in printed reviews, without the prior permission of the author or publisher.

ISBN-13: 978-1517518271
ISBN-10: 151751B27X

All passages unless otherwise stated are taken from the
New International Version of the Bible; BibleGateway.com
Copyright © 1995-2006 Gospel Communications International;
http://www.biblegateway.com

Share your story with the author or request information at:
info@fortune5ministries.com
www.fortune5ministries.com

Presented to: _____

From: _____

Date: _____

Welcome Message

The book in your hands is fun to read. More importantly, it will help you to put your faith into action – and it will help grow greater faith within your children, too. We all know that Jesus really is the reason for the season, but how do we help our children understand this, especially in today's world, where commercialism runs rampant?

This story of a special young boy who shares his feelings with his family, and makes Christmas even more special, will make it easier than ever to carry out your faith and live according to God's word.

Your children will learn just how real their faith can be when they hear how much more the boy's family enjoy Christmas Day. The fellowship they share by taking the time to celebrate the guest of honor – Jesus – by baking a beautiful birthday cake, singing "Happy Birthday," and giving Jesus gifts from their hearts has become a beautiful family tradition.

Narrative Reflections Worksheet

Throughout this book, there will be opportunities to pause and reflect on scripture and ideas that highlight the book's narrative. In the back of the book, you will find a Narrative Reflections Worksheet that provides you an opportunity to capture your answers to the questions posed throughout the book. There's also a journal to capture the thoughts, feelings and ideas you had as you read the book.

Acknowledgements

I first thank God, my Lord of Host, for the vision He planted in me to write this story. Thank you to my family for allowing me to share this wonderful tradition with the world. An extraordinary thanks to my God-fearing son Zachary, who was insistent upon understanding and practicing the true meaning of Christmas.

Loving thanks go to my amazing husband, Terry who has supported me in this endeavor, and my two beautiful daughters Zéah and Zuriana who graciously critiqued each spread.

Sincere thanks to my dear friend, Shakir McDonald, who encouraged me to step off the cliff and allow God to do the rest. Special thanks to Jeremy Guy and Karen Murphy, who took time to proofread and edit the story. Special thanks also to my Pastor, Dr. Bernard T. Fuller who ensured a clear message of the gospel is presented. A distinctive thanks goes to Bryan Ramos, the one who helped turn my dream into a reality, he saw it clearly and encouraged me to keep moving despite the hiccups along the way. Big thanks to all of you who patiently waited for this project to be completed, consistently encouraged me, and were 1st in line to get your copy! I am forever grateful to you all!

What is Christmas all about?
I am still young and trying to figure it out.

Reflection: What does Christmas mean to you?

She will give birth to a son, and you are to give Him the name Jesus, because He will save His people from their sins. Matthew 1:21

For to us a child is born, to us a son is given, and the government will be on his shoulders. And He will be called Wonderful Counselor, Mighty God, Everlasting Father, Prince of Peace. Isaiah 9:6

I wake up one day and see toys under the tree.
Mom and Dad are smiling, just watching over me.

My eyes go wide when I see the things that are new.
What next, I wonder; what am I supposed to do?

Reflection: What's your favorite gift?

Every good and perfect gift is from above, coming down from the Father of the heavenly lights, who does not change like shifting shadows. James 1:17

"Merry Christmas, Zach!" both my smiling parents yell.
I'm still confused, but this will be great, I can tell.

"What is with all the toys?" I ask them with a sigh.
"Because it is Jesus' birthday!" they reply.

"Wow, Jesus got all these cool things? Can I play too?"
"Oh, Zach, don't you see? These toys are here just for you!"

Reflection: What's the best gift you've ever given, or would like to give?

Each of you should use whatever gift you have received to serve others, as faithful stewards of God's grace in its various forms. 1 Peter 4:10

I begin to question all of this in my mind.
Why aren't those toys for Jesus? Wouldn't that be kind?

On birthdays, there are things that always make me smile.
We sing, eat cake, open gifts and play for a while.

The kitchen has cake, but not a candle in sight.
If there is no candle, then what are we to light?

Reflection: Do you have faith when things don't seem to be going your way?

And without faith it is impossible to please Him, for he who comes to God must believe that He is, and that He is a rewarder of those who seek Him. Hebrews 11:6

Later, some of my aunts, uncles, cousins and more,
Come carrying gifts and laughter through the front door.

Is there one gift with Jesus' name on the tag,
Maybe all of his gifts are in another bag?

Reflection: Do you show God's Love to your family and friends?

Dear friends, let us love one another, for love comes from God. Everyone who loves has been born of God and knows God. 1 John 4:7

It's time to eat and we all bow our heads to pray,
"Thank you, Dear Lord, for giving us this precious day…"

Reflection: Do you remember to say Thank You to God and others?

Give thanks in all circumstances; for this is God's will for you in Christ Jesus.
1 Thessalonians 5:18

At dessert, I think they finally remember,
Jesus was born on this great day in December!

No songs? But they all grab a slice of cake or pie.
"So they did forget?" I say, with tears in my eyes.

Reflection: How would you feel if no one acknowledged it was your birthday?

The righteous cry out, and the LORD hears them; he delivers them from all their troubles. The LORD is close to the brokenhearted and saves those who are crushed in spirit. Psalm 34: 17-18

"Mom, I'm confused. Am I the only one awake?"
"It's Jesus' birthday! Where is His birthday cake?

Where are all the birthday songs we usually sing?
Jesus' gifts – did anyone bring Him a thing?"

Reflection: Do you ever feel like no one is listening to you?

You, Lord, hear the desire of the afflicted, you encourage them, and you listen to their cry.   Psalm 10:17

My mommy says, "Oh, honey, aren't you just so sweet. What are the kinds of gifts Jesus would think are neat?"

"Well, I doubt that he wants toys, games, gloves or a hat. He wants us to give love, joy and peace… stuff like that."

Why don't we give Jesus what's truly in our hearts? Isn't that a wonderful place for us to start?

Reflection: Does Jesus have a place in your heart?

But the fruit of the Spirit is love, joy, peace, forbearance, kindness, goodness, faithfulness, gentleness and self-control. Against such things there is no law. Galatians 5:22-23

"We will write them down and put them under the tree.
He'll be excited to get gifts from you and me!"

I smile as each family member writes a note.
Then listen as each one shares the caring things they wrote.

Some give their heart and vow to spend more time with Him,
Others reflect and give things that are dear to them.

Reflection: Did you know that God can use you to share His word at any age?

Don't let anyone look down on you because you are young, but set an example for the believers in speech, in conduct, in love, in faith and in purity. 1 Timothy 4:12

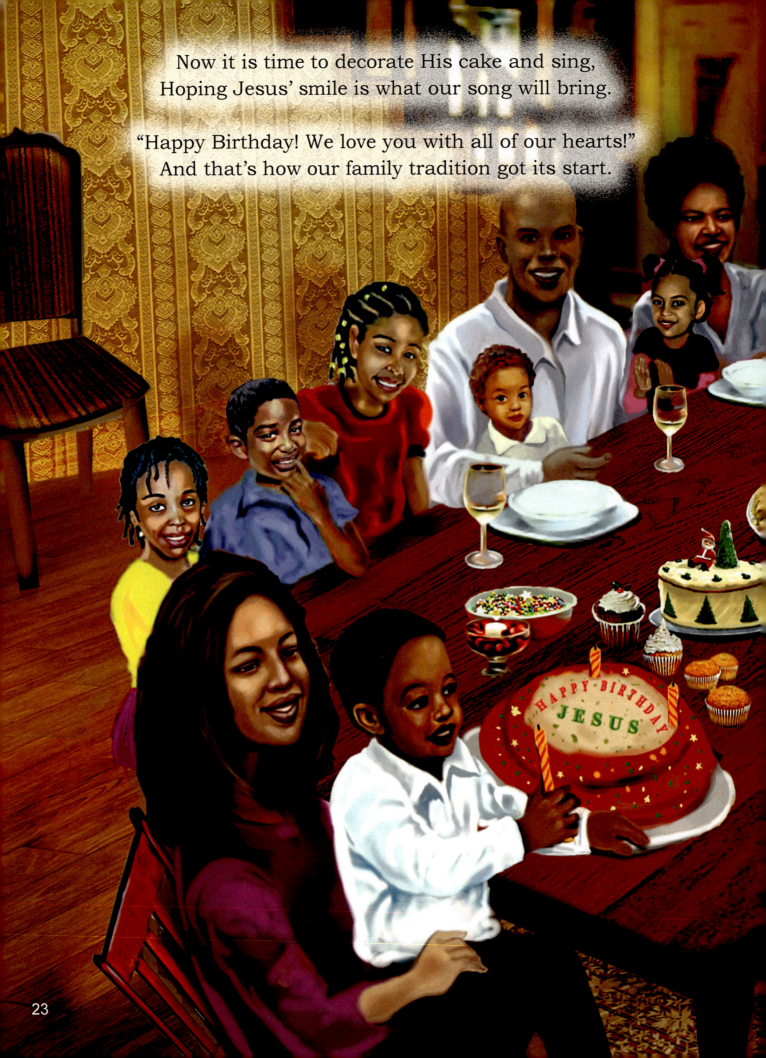

Now it is time to decorate His cake and sing,
Hoping Jesus' smile is what our song will bring.

"Happy Birthday! We love you with all of our hearts!"
And that's how our family tradition got its start.

Reflection: How do you celebrate Christmas?

Today in the town of David a Savior has been born to you; He is the Messiah, the Lord. Luke 2:11

Every year since that magnificent Christmas day,
Our family celebrated a whole new way.

Cake and sincere gifts from our hearts, Jesus receives,
And salvation is His gift, to all who believe.

Reflections: Are you willing to receive the greatest gift of all?

For the wages of sin is death, but the gift of God is eternal life in Christ Jesus our Lord. Romans 6:23

For God so loved the world that he gave His only Son, that whoever believes in Him shall not perish but have eternal life. John 3:16

If you declare with your mouth, "Jesus is Lord," and believe in your heart that God raised him from the dead, you will be saved. For it is with your heart that you believe and are justified, and it is with your mouth that you profess your faith and are saved. Romans 10:9-10

For it is by grace you have been saved, through faith—and this is not from yourselves, it is the gift of God. Ephesians 2:8

Narrative Reflections Worksheet

Page 4
Reflection: What does Christmas mean to you?
_____
_____

She will give birth to a son, and you are to give Him the name Jesus, because He will save His people from their sins. Matthew 1:21

For to us a child is born, to us a son is given, and the government will be on his shoulders. And He will be called Wonderful Counselor, Mighty God, Everlasting Father, Prince of Peace. Isaiah 9:6

Page 6
Reflection: What's your favorite gift?
_____
_____

Every good and perfect gift is from above, coming down from the Father of the heavenly lights, who does not change like shifting shadows. James 1:17

Page 8
Reflection: What's the best gift you've ever given, or would like to give?
_____
_____

Each of you should use whatever gift you have received to serve others, as faithful stewards of God's grace in its various forms. 1 Peter 4:10

Page 10
Reflection: Do you have faith when things don't seem to be going your way?
_____
_____

And without faith it is impossible to please Him, for he who comes to God must believe that He is, and that He is a rewarder of those who seek Him. Hebrews 11:6

Page 12
Reflection: Do you show God's Love to your family and friends?
_____
_____

Dear friends, let us love one another, for love comes from God. Everyone who loves has been born of God and knows God. 1 John 4:7

Page 14
Reflection: Do you remember to say Thank You to God and others?
_____
_____

Give thanks in all circumstances; for this is God's will for you in Christ Jesus. 1 Thessalonians 5:18

Page 16
Reflection: How would you feel if no one acknowledged it was your birthday?
_____
_____

The righteous cry out, and the LORD hears them; he delivers them from all their troubles. The LORD is close to the brokenhearted and saves those who are crushed in spirit. Psalm 34: 17-18

Page 18
Reflection: Do you ever feel like no one is listening to you?
_____
_____

You, Lord, hear the desire of the afflicted, you encourage them, and you listen to their cry. Psalm 10:17

Page 20
Reflection: Does Jesus have a place in your heart?
_____
_____

But the fruit of the Spirit is love, joy, peace, forbearance, kindness, goodness, faithfulness, gentleness and self-control. Against such things there is no law. Galatians 5:22-23

Page 22
Reflection: Did you know that God can use you to share His word at any age?
_____
_____

Don't let anyone look down on you because you are young, but set an example for the believers in speech, in conduct, in love, in faith and in purity. 1 Timothy 4:12

Page 24
Reflection: How do you celebrate Christmas?
_____
_____

Today in the town of David a Savior has been born to you; He is the Messiah, the Lord. Luke 2:11

Page 26
Reflections: Are you willing to receive the greatest gift of all?
_____
_____

For the wages of sin is death, but the gift of God is eternal life in Christ Jesus our Lord. Romans 6:23

For God so loved the world that he gave His only Son, that whoever believes in Him shall not perish but have eternal life. John 3:16

If you declare with your mouth, "Jesus is Lord," and believe in your heart that God raised him from the dead, you will be saved. For it is with your heart that you believe and are justified, and it is with your mouth that you profess your faith and are saved. Romans 10:9-10

For it is by grace you have been saved, through faith—and this is not from yourselves, it is the gift of God. Ephesians 2:8

Your Faith Journal

Feel free to use the space below to capture thoughts, feelings and ideas you had as you read this book and worked through the reflections. Our prayer is that this book helped you to deepen your relationship with Jesus and that you learned some practical ways to practice your faith in this world. Thank you for being you.

_____
_____
_____
_____
_____
_____
_____
_____
_____
_____
_____
_____
_____
_____
_____
_____
_____
_____
_____
_____
_____
_____
_____
_____

Your Faith Journal

Closing Thoughts...

Christmas is a special time with family, friends and the guest of honor Christ. Make this the best Christmas ever and receive the most cherished gift of all... Christ Himself.

Thanks be to God for His indescribable gift.
2 Corinthians 9:15

Celebrate the true meaning of Christmas.

Our lights are shining bright on our houses and our trees, for all to see! Let's ensure "The Light" (Jesus) is shining bright through you and me!

For God, who said, "Let light shine out of darkness," made his light shine in our hearts to give us the light of the knowledge of God's glory displayed in the face of Christ.
2 Corinthians 4:6

For you were once darkness, but now you are light in the Lord. Live as children of light.
Ephesians 5:8

About the Author

Monica Fortune is a loving wife and mother of three wonderful children. Her faith in God is unwavering, always standing on the promise of God that everything works together for good for those who love the Lord and are called according to His purpose. This became the basis in her life following her mother's death when Monica was 16 years old, which was the start of her relationship with God. She is an active member of her church where she has served as Nursery Director, Children's Church Coordinator, Disciple's LIFE Assistant Director, Assistant Care Group Leader, Sunday School Teacher and a Leader of a Girl's Mentoring Ministry (God's Precious Jewels). She is also a published author in *Halo Magazine*.

Made in the USA
Middletown, DE
30 October 2015